MW00653221

Saving Singletrees

BY Leo Dangel

Wayne, Nebraska 68787
wscpress@wsc.edu

Saving Singletrees

ISBN: 978-0-9823828-8-2

Book #9 of the Kloefkorn Series
Kloefkorn Series Copyright © 2013 WSC Press

Editing, Layout, and Design, Tyisha Wrice
Managing Editor, Chad Christensen

WSC Press
Wayne, NE 68787
wsc.edu/wscpress
wscpress@wsc.edu

Printed in the United States by McNaughton & Gunn
960 Woodland Drive
Saline, MI 48176
734.429.5411

Saving Singletrees

In memory of Bill Holm,
a master at capturing
in prose and poetry
a place and its inhabitants.

TABLE OF CONTENTS

III. Tapping the Line of Memory

IV. Dancing the Green Two-Step

singletree ... *n.* The pivoted horizontal crossbar to which the harness traces of a draft animal are attached and which is in turn attached to a vehicle or an implement.

—The American Heritage Dictionary

What is the shame for human beings to weep at the passage of time and feel it in the disappearance of the objects of our past? These emotions give us all literature and music and art. They give us our humanity.

—Bill Holm, The Windows of Brimnes

Plowing Furrows
in the Clouds

Starting the Day

The tin can, serving as a rain hat
on the muffler of the John Deere,
is delighted when the farmer forgets
to remove it. That first engine pop
sends the old pork 'n' bean can
flying in a joyous blue-sky arc
to land sprawled and laughing
on the soft wet grass.

Seasons of Harmony

The motor of my Super-M
hummed at the right pitch,
and the three-bottom plow
scoured in the wet stubble
as I cruised in third gear
into the night to finish up
the spring plowing;
traveling along with me
just above my shoulder,
a plowshare crescent moon
turned furrows in the clouds.

Essentials of Comedy

My father and I were milking.
A cow with a case of scours
was relieving herself, a stream
of soupy green shit pouring down
out of her rump. As a rule,
one should avoid passing behind
the animal when this is happening,
but my father, carrying a pail
of milk, did inadvertently walk
past the cow, about eight feet
behind her, at which time
she also had an urge to cough.

No one could dream up a situation
with so much comic potential,
and my father's line of curses
was magnificent, long and intense,
but I couldn't laugh. Even now
I can barely muster a smile as I recall
how helpless he was going out
to the water tank to wash his shirt
and the milk pail—his only revenge
on the cow who'd drink the water.

I was left without a good joke to tell
unless I'd change a few details:
My father and I were milking,
and a congressman walked into the barn . . .

Convergence

As a youth I combed my hair in waves
and swirls with a part like a furrow
plowed through a field of long grass
that curled over and lay flat in curves,
harrowed into place around the sides
and down the back, shaped, sculptured,
and tamed by Wildroot Cream Oil,
while my father had his hair cut short
and let it go its own way, ignoring it
except for occasions like Sundays,
when he spent not even a minute
before church combing it with water
in directions it wanted to go, about
the same way I wear my hair now.

Screech Owl

I picked up a clump of feathers,
which looked like the remains of a bird
beside the cats' milk dish in the barn,
but the head turned slowly, the eyes
opened and stared fiercely into mine,
as if to say, "Don't mess with me."
The silent little owl seemed to screech
a warning or threat I shouldn't ignore.

This night creature, smaller than my fist,
apparently chose to rest for the day
in a dim corner of the barn, among
half a dozen cats waiting to be fed,
or a cat had brought it there to eat later,
and it was taking a nap before escaping—
I had to admire that kind of audacity.

Although the owl appeared unhurt,
I wasn't sure about its safety,
and I carried it out to an evergreen tree,
placing it gently on a branch. Returning
to chores, I glanced back and saw
it fly off into the shadows of the grove,
away from my human meddling,
probably seeking a place less bright—
the dark to an owl must seem like light.

The Bouquet He Saved for Her

He comes in from the field at noon
and stands in the kitchen, looking shy,
holding out to me a bunch of wild roses,
yellow mustard flowers, and purple
thistle blooms with the stems
wrapped in his blue handkerchief.

"Do you have a jar or something
to put these in? Be careful now,
they're sharp, but they looked so nice
I cut a few with my pocket knife."

Of course they're weeds—he'll spray
the rest soon—but, still, they're lovely.

It

He's worn the thing for years.
It's a brown cotton sweatshirt,
long, with buttons down the front,
ragged around the cuffs and bottom,
full of holes the size of pennies,
and usually it's embedded with dirt.
I seldom wash it—he thinks some
of the sweatshirt is lost when I do.

He wears it on cool days and adds
a coat for the extra-cold ones.
Today he went out and left it hanging
on its hook—the coat was enough.
The kitchen was chilly, and I didn't
have a sweater handy. I put it on.

I have to admit it kept me warm,
and I almost forgot I was wearing it
as I went about mixing the dough
to make bread. I suppose I should
throw the thing out, but he insists
we'll never find another one like it.
I might as well wait. Sooner or later
it has to disintegrate—never mind
if it takes its sweet old time.

Frozen Washdays

Everything depends on my mother,
the master of an old Maytag wringer
washing machine with a gas motor.
She adjusts screws on the carburetor
and steps down on the kick starter.
The small entryway, serving as laundry,
is cold—the door is open enough
to let the motor's flexible exhaust pipe
poke through and billow clouds
of white smoke into the frigid air.

Standing on a layer of hard snow,
bare-handed, she hangs wet clothes
that'll freeze before they're half dry.
She carries in sheets stacked up
like boards on her arms.
Cords strung across the living room
hold a crowd of thawing laundry.
Standing stiffly against the wall,
helpless long johns need to be rescued
before they collapse on the floor.

Independent Harvesters

If our oats crop was ripe on the 4th of July,
there was no liberty for us. My father pulled
the grain binder out from its place under
a cottonwood tree, the sickle sharpened and fierce.

Our uniform was faded cotton and straw hats.
My mother drove the rusty tractor, and my father
operated the binder, the sickle rattling back
and forth, sounding like a machine gun,
mowing down the standing grain in its path.
My sisters and I set the bundles into shocks
that covered the field in rows of monuments.

No one thought of Washington or flags.
I remember the taste of the water,
kept cool in a Mason jar under a shock,
and how the stubble felt when it broke
under my soles. The hemp twine that tied
our harvest together had a certain smell.

We saw the late sun slanting on the field.

A Failed Landmark

Out in the field, taken for granted,
the abandoned corn picker and a willow
growing up through it were both gone
one day—someone needed more land.

A Farming Life

As a young horse in the pasture,
you had always vaguely assumed
you'd wear the harness and pull
a cultivator or plow, a hard
life's work but an easy choice.
You only had to keep on doing
the work your father had done,
the work you'd already begun.

There was that one time,
beside the creek, where it runs
under the fence, you noticed
the top strand of barbed wire
between two posts was broken.
You wondered if you might
be able to jump the fence there—
a good stretch of even ground
for a running start to the jump,
then follow the creek. It had
to lead somewhere. You thought
about it for a day, but, by the next
evening, the fence had been fixed.

And now you're in the barn
on a winter night, your tired bones
chilling in a drafty stall. Not sleeping,
you dream of a springtime pasture
that shines in frosty moonlight.
You see the broken wire, the barbs
glinting like tiny Christmas lights.

The fence looks terribly low.
One easy jump,
and you would have been gone.

Lights

Not many farms were west of ours
After dark, if we saw a car light
come from the south and turn west
at our corner, chances were good
someone was coming to visit us.

Now, I have less use for other kinds
of lights—I don't look for the light
at the end of the tunnel, or for a beacon
of hope to guide me, and I can't picture
what could light up the whole world.

I'm happy when I catch a glimmer
off to the side and moving toward
the corner of my eye. I'll slowly turn
my head that way. Maybe the light
will slow down, getting itself ready

to turn and sweep over a field.

On Being a Squirter

And the milk that squirts
from one mystery to
another, and back
somehow...

—William Kloefkorn, poem 29
in his book *Alvin Turner as Farmer.*

Like Alvin Turner, I am a squirter
of milk into the mouths of cats.
When I've finished milking this cow,
I'll pour some milk into the cats' dish,
and they'll lap it up with their delicate,
pink tongues in the usual way and find
it good, but now the calico cat sits
three feet away, waiting, anticipating
the milk I'll squirt into her mouth.
Why do I do it? I can't help myself.
There's something about delivering
the sustenance of life in a different way—
sending it flying through air,
directly into a mouth—so efficient
and yet so delightfully circus-like.
And then there's the cat—the cat needs
no teaching but knows in an instant
to drink the milk coming at her face.
It doesn't matter if some drops miss—
the cat will find and appreciate
those later when licking her fur.
I think what I do must be like squeezing

a wineskin and squirting a vintage stream
into the mouth of someone, a lover perhaps.
Or maybe it'd be like squeezing a poem
somehow and sending forth streams
of words—all of you, eat, drink, inhale,
paw your faces and lick in every drop.

Grocery String

Those were the days
of groceries wrapped
like presents in sheets
of brown paper from rolls
and tied up with cotton string,
Cheerios, crackers, cheese,
and cans of Spam and salmon
brought home in a package
from town or country store,
and then the unwrapping,
a little bit like a celebration,
the paper folded, saved,
the string, too, wound
on a ball and kept in a drawer,
string you could break off
in a certain needed length
until time and bags, plastic
or paper, unwound it all,
and you came to the end
of the grocery-string ball.

Dakota Wind

As I was walking home
from school in winter, it took
away my breath. Sometimes
I walked backwards not to face it.

In spring, when I rode
my Hiawatha bike, it seldom
seemed to be at my back.

If I was driving a tractor in the field,
it blew from the side, over the tire,
peeling off grains of dirt that stung
my face and packed my ears.

But now, after so many years,
when the scent of fall grass
and ripe corn comes to me
on a strong wind, I just lean

into it, happy to breathe it in.

Saving Singletrees

Reading *The Grapes of Wrath* during
an afternoon high-school study hall,
I was mostly in an empty farmyard
at twilight with the Joad family
at the beginning of a journey.

They've sold all the farm implements
and gear. Needing a food supply
for on the road, they're getting ready
to butcher a couple of pigs. Pa says,
"Shouldn't of sold those singletrees."

This was talk I understood.
Pleased to be an insider, I knew
that a singletree, a wooden crossbar
with hooks on the ends for hitching
a horse to a load, is also quite handy

for butchering. I had seen men
put the hooks of a singletree under the
hind-leg tendons of a slaughtered pig
and hoist it up for scalding, gutting,
and scraping the bristles off the skin.

Years later, as I'm reading the novel,
the familiar farm details capture me
all over again, but now I'm reminded
how I've lost, given up, or discarded
things I'd wish too late I had kept.

When my aging parents sold the farm,
I should have asked them to save me
a singletree. Who knows what uses
I'd find for it? It might stand for all
of the things I long to have back,

and, if I had a singletree to show off,
I'd have occasions to say the word:
"Singletree"—I've always liked the sound
of it—a musical harkening back
to a live tree with branches and roots.

Navigating
Chocolate Rivers

The Evidence of Pleasure

On Saturday night going home
from Turkey Ridge Store,
while my father drives,
I'm leaning out of my window
and eating a tasty Fudgesicle
as I watch grassy fence lines
and groves of trees roll by.
I'm taking in the darkness, too,
the different, cleaner smell
of night, and a cooling wind
because the car is moving.

On Sunday morning the sun is hot
when all of us are in the car,
leaving for church, and, because
the girls don't want a breeze
of any sort messing up their hair,
my mother rolls up the window
I left open, which now looks like
a sticky map of chocolate rivers.

When I Was Small

Maybe I could have loved
our shabby '34 Ford
if I had only known
it was the getaway car
of choice for bank robbers
Bonnie and Clyde.

My golden dime-store ring
turned a dirty green.
Our car was that color.

Once, at my uncle's farm,
my father, busy talking,
forgot I'd come along
and drove off without me.
He'd remember and come back.
We would have better cars,

but I ran after that one.

My First Memory of Dancing

My sisters taught me,
their only brother, to dance.
I remember Monica
stopped cleaning the kitchen
one afternoon to practice
with me. She hummed
a song, and we moved
on the yellow linoleum
in the space between
table and stove, cupboard,
sink and sewing machine.

This dancing, I trusted,
was a good thing to learn
and worth serious attention.
I wish I knew how to thank
all of my sisters for their gift,
one I would appreciate
as a self-conscious teenager.

The gift, though, was best
while it was first being given,
before I had any idea
what grace was.

Tasting the Past

While eating a square
from a chocolate bar,
I absentmindedly
bite into a soda cracker
left lying on the table,
and I'm tasting again
a crispy-moist,
starchy-chocolate,
salty-sweet
Saturday afternoon,
when my sister, Mary,
putting the finishing
touches on a cake,
layers left-over
chocolate frosting
between soda crackers
and sets down
a plateful of them
in front of me.

In My First-Grade Coloring Book

The wife of Peter, Peter, pumpkin eater,
is in a pumpkin, where he keeps her.
Her face is all that shows in the window.
What color should I use? I don't know.

My little box of crayons has no color
that seems right for a face—I pick yellow.
I think it's the best one I have for skin,
and orange is just right for the pumpkin.

The teacher scolds me, "Yellow's not right.
You should have just left her face white."
I can't explain how I tried to do a good job
and not my usual sloppy work. I feel bad,

but I still think yellow is good for a face—
inside the orange pumpkin, it looks nice.

A Country-School Teacher

Today I had to confiscate
a thread spool with a wooden pin
nicely whittled to fit inside
and powered by rubber bands
strung tightly on notches
carved into the spool's edges,
a device clearly contrived
for launching spit wads,
likely not effective, except
perhaps at point-blank range,
concealable in hand or pocket,
as weapons go, a derringer,
but still a fine miniature work
by an inspired twelve-year-old.

Poetry Lesson

The teacher at our country school
told everyone to write a poem
and read it at the front of the room.

Of a dozen poems, including mine,
I can remember only the one
Duane, a third grader, wrote:

"I have a skunk, and he is black.
I like to play with him,
and he likes to play in the haystack."

The teacher praised Duane's poem.
We all liked it, too, even though
we knew he didn't have a skunk.

The Artist as a Young Man

The visiting astronomer set up a model
of the solar system in the high-school gym.
The sun, at center court, was surrounded
by five planets on long rods like the spokes
of a wheel. An electric motor and gears
made the planets circle around the sun,
the earth spin on its axis, and the moon
orbit the earth. He said there wasn't room
for all nine planets but that this basic model
represented how the solar system worked.

Explaining old theories that said everything
revolved around the earth, he pointed out
that there would be no way to account
for how heavenly bodies appear to move
if the earth were located at the center.

An idea occurred to me. I said, "Suppose
you had an iron shaft come straight down
from the ceiling, and you clamped the earth
tight to the end of the shaft so that it held
the whole machine off of the floor.
Then, if you switched on the motor, the sun
and planets would, more or less, circle
around the earth fixed solid at the center.
It'd be like when you hold a wind-up toy car
by one wheel—the whole car spins around."

The astronomer said my idea was ridiculous,
but my classmates laughed and murmured

as if they saw that I was onto something.
Of course I knew there had to be problems
with my hypothesis—I'd guess that Jupiter
would have been whizzing around in orbit
at somewhere beyond the speed of light.

I've always admired and liked science,
but, as we all watched and believed the neat,
pokey model, I think that most preferred
my picture of the whole rigmarole gone wild,
gyrating around the earth—I was glad
I'd brought the whole thing up.

The Raspy Wheel

Babe and Beauty, our last team of horses,
were old like the full rickety hayrack
they were pulling home from the little field
of prairie hay in a corner of our farm.

The old-fashioned wheels, without bearings,
turned on iron sleeves over wooden axles.
One front wheel, for want of grease, screeched
all the way to the creek, where we stopped.

My father said, "We'll let the horses rest
before we go across." The creek was as dry
as the wheel, but hauling the heavy load
up the opposite bank would still be hard.

It was quiet. I heard the wings of a dragonfly,
the swish of a horse's tail, my father's
gentle "Giddy-up," and the grating wheel
turning again, down into the creek bed,

up the other side and a long, gradual hill
before the pasture. The screeching kept time
to the horses' pace and sank into my memory.
If the raspy wheel had been greased,

I might have forgotten the whole afternoon.

The Girl I Saw at a Movie

I was thirteen, alone in my row
at a movie, when I glanced around
and saw a pretty dark-haired girl
sitting directly behind me. I soon
turned again. Looking above her,
I pretended to scan the theater
as if searching for someone
in the back, but I slanted my gaze
downward enough to see her.
Flanked by two faceless friends,
she was alone, different, having
a beauty I'd never seen before.
Her bright, shining eyes watched
the movie, one I don't remember
though I watched it, too, for a while
until I couldn't resist turning
to steal another look. I repeated
my fake search of the theater
and saw her for the last time.
She was still mysterious and lovely,
even when she pointed to the screen
and said, "Hey, the show's up there."

When Cuffs Were Fashionable

Even while doing farm work
I wore my jeans rolled up,
stylishly collecting dirt.

Legion Baseball, 1957

It was the first game I got to start.
Playing left field, I didn't quite get
in front of an easy fly and had to reach

down and to my left. The ball,
I swear, was in the pocket of my glove,
and then it was falling to the ground.

At the end of the inning, our manager,
a tall wiry man named Rosie,
was not at all rosy when he met me

in front of the bench. "You," he said,
"get both hands on the ball—
you're not Willie Mays yet."

That "yet" had a bitter bite to it,
implying I was cocky enough to think
I was the next Willie Mays, and, yet,

I clearly would never be a Willie Mays,
and Rosie might have said so.
I could sort of appreciate the "yet."

My Pioneer Grandmother

As a boy of fourteen, I inherited
my grandmother's slippers.
When she died, the family
divided up some of her things
that no one seemed to want,
and my parents brought home
a few of her belongings. I saw
the slippers and wanted them.
They were actually moccasins,
well worn, made of cheap
buckskin-colored leather,
likely in a 1950s factory,
but they at least looked
authentic and fit me perfectly.
I felt like Davy Crockett.

It didn't occur to me
my grandmother grew up
on the prairie in the 1880s
and was kind of a hero, too.
I recall little about her.
She was short, stout,
had brown eyes and black hair
that never turned gray.
Her words had a German flavor.
I remember she pronounced
the word "mouth" as "mout."
The minute you entered her house
she was bringing you food.
She gave us kids coffee

with lots of cream and sugar.

Grandma, now in my daydreams
I'm putting on your slippers
once again, not because
of their look of frontier adventure
but because they were yours.

In Gratitude for Apples

There were always apples in the pantry;
I could have one anytime, and yet
an apple in the toe of my Christmas stocking
was always, mysteriously, still a gift.

Apples are now my usual evening snack.
Someone urges me to try a new variety
that smells and tastes like grapes—it does,
a little, but some apple taste gets lost

in a watery flavor mix that is no gift.
The few small apples from the trees
in a meager orchard my parents planted
before I can remember were better.

We had cherries and larger apples, good
for pies, but those small Whitney crabapples
I ate right from the trees in late summer
provided an original flavor so tempting

I pictured Eve smuggling a forbidden seedling
out of Eden, concealing it under her fig-leaf clothes.

The Chance I Missed

Reading *A Field Guide to Edible Wild Plants*,
I wondered if I could have eaten
the abundant weeds around our farm.
I would have liked living off the land
without planting or lifting a hoe
and regretted missing out
on something basic and satisfying.

Of course we picked wild plums
and chokecherries that my mother
turned into delicious jams and jellies.
But eating milkweeds, wild roses,
cattails, pigweeds, or goat's beard
was beyond anything I imagined.
The book says some wild plants
are quite tasty served raw in salads.

Then, turning a page, I recalled
something Aunt Mary once said
about living through drought
and hard times: "We had to eat
the thistles growing in the pasture."
I recognized the bull thistle
in the color picture, the spiny leaves
and purple blooms, a pretty plant
but not one you'd want to touch
or likely think of eating. Because
of the spines, the guide book advises,
"You may prefer to use thistles only
as a survival food." Thistles usually

require boiling, changing the water
once or twice to remove bitterness.

I never thought to ask Aunt Mary
about what led them to eat these things,
or how they ever learned they could.

What They Carried

Later, the pallbearers,
all farm boys, talked quietly
about the unexpected heaviness
of their classmate's casket.
Each one's share of weight,
they agreed, felt like
a five-gallon pail of water.

Tapping the Line of Memory

His Refund on Her Plans

My wife had shopping bags full of yarn
banked up in a corner of the bedroom,
almost enough to reach the moon.
She insisted she needed all of it for vests
and sweaters she had promised to knit
for relatives. She had plans for afghans.

When she died, the pile of yarn was still there.
My daughters didn't know what to do with it,
but, after a few weeks alone, I needed
to do something—I loaded the yarn
into the pickup and took it back to Alco.

She had bought yarn there for the last
two or three years but kept no receipts.
I don't know what the clerks thought.
I said, "My wife bought this yarn—she died,
and I can't knit." They took back all of it.

As they tallied up the skeins, I noticed
the bright colors—I wish I could see
what she had in mind for them.
I didn't like seeing the yarn go back,
and the money wasn't important.

I was thankful, anyway, for every one
of her unfinished plans.
She never could have had too many,
and they all turned out to be free.

She Remembers His Overalls

On Sunday evening, when he wore dress pants
to go visiting, and we came home not long
before bedtime, out of habit he'd put on
his overalls just to sit and read a magazine.
He wasn't at home wearing anything else.

It took awhile before a new pair of overalls
was really his. I had to wash them until
they faded a little before they felt good
to him. The tool pocket on the leg wore thin
from his pliers. A faded circle started to show
on the left back pocket from a box of snuff,
and another circle appeared on the chest pocket,
where, tied to a shoestring, he kept a watch
he'd forget to wind. It often stood still.

But even apart from the smaller marks
and the patches I sewed on the knees,
his overalls had lines and a shape I'd know
close up and from a distance. There's a pair
left in the entryway hanging by the suspenders.

The Watkins Man

About once every other month, he came
to our farm. His black Chevy panel-truck,
resembling a small hearse, had a door
in back that opened to a wonderful
blended smell of spices and extracts.

He'd come into the kitchen with a crate
of his wares and sit in the chair by the door.
My mother was a loyal customer for things
she'd never buy in stores—vanilla, pepper,
cinnamon, and other spices and flavors.

His voice had sort of a cry in it.
I believe he sounded like Pat Buttram,
Gene Autry's sidekick, without the humor.
But I remember the smells of what he sold
more than the man—they were on him, too.

If my mother asked for a special item,
he'd go back out to get it from his truck.
I'd follow along to see inside and take in
the full scent when the back door swung open.
I've forgotten his name, which I heard

spoken only once, when my mother
said it in reporting that he had died.
My father said, "Who?"
"The Watkins Man."
"Oh."

The Pinochle Players

After supper my sisters and I played
four-handed pinochle with our parents
around the kitchen table. We enjoyed
the variety of changing partners,
taking turns as players or spectators,
sitting in for someone who decided
to go and make popcorn.

The youngest and last to leave home,
I played three-handed with my mother
and father, still a good game, one settled
into an established trio but changing
with every hand, when two players
found it in their own interests
to team up against the third.

In their last years, alone on many nights,
they discovered they still could play.
Pinochle was certainly never intended
for two-handed play, with more cards
in the deck than two people can hold,
but they designed their own rules
using a large kitty or blind and discards.
I didn't see how it could be much fun,
always a routine one-on-one competition
and little mystery, once play started,
about what cards the other player held.

It had to be more than liking the game
or keeping a tradition. I know that finding

they could play two-handed pleased them,
and maybe they'd found a way to forestall
thinking about the time when one of them
would be alone with the unthinkable,
the game of pinochle as solitaire.

Gestures in the Garden

My Danish mother, Lutheran turned Catholic,
is standing in the garden between the rows
and having an argument with her brother Carl,
a Lutheran turned Witness of Jehovah.

From my position, out of hearing range,
I know the subject's not the cabbage crop.
Her lively gestures tell me this exchange
concerns religion—Carl's favorite topic.

He always claims the world's about to end.
For proof he pulls a paper from his pocket,
but, waving off the text, she shakes her head.
Taking her vegetables gathered in a basket,

she holds the earthly part of her religion
and points the way to heaven with an onion.

Audible Silence

On the wall by the nurse's desk,
there's an alarm panel behind glass.
A note, taped to the glass, reads,
"If you silence any alarm on this panel
or find it alarming, call maintenance."
The panel displays various alarms:
"SECURITY," "POWER," and one I find
strangely familiar, "AUDIBLE SILENCE."

Twenty-five years ago, a TV sitcom,
one I never could stand to watch,
came on when my sister called
to tell me our mother had died.
Her death was expected and came
quietly, but, still, the news settled
like a heavy droning in my head.

After hanging up, I switched
the TV off. A silence followed
and fixed itself in my memory
of the moment with background
clowning voices I'll always hear,
because I carelessly left a TV on.

There's no use calling maintenance.
I sometimes find audible silence
alarming, or discomforting at least.
The trouble is I can't silence it.

In Memoriam

In the early afternoon my mother
was doing the dishes. I climbed
onto the kitchen table, I suppose
to play, and fell asleep there.
I was drowsy and awake, though,
as she lifted me up, carried me
on her arms into the living room,
and placed me on the davenport,
but I pretended to be asleep
the whole time, enjoying the luxury—
I was too big for such a privilege
and just old enough to form
my only memory of her carrying me.
She's still moving me to a softer place.

Reporting at My Father's Grave

Nowadays you'd hardly recognize
the farm machinery. A computer
drives the tractor, and a satellite
in space tells the computer where
to go in the field. The farmer rides
along in an air-conditioned cab
and watches how everything works.

I think about your old tractor,
the 10-20 with its lugged wheels
and wide front end. It steered hard,
but, when you plowed, the two wheels
on one side stayed in the furrow,
and no steering was needed.

I remember you enjoyed telling
how you once got off the tractor
and sent it plowing in low gear
through a nest of angry bumblebees,
while you walked around to the end
of the field to get on again.

That was the first tractor I drove.
You were plowing in the field
west of the barn with me on your lap.
I took the steering wheel with both
hands and wiggled it left and right.
I wasn't strong enough to steer
off course, but we were plowing,
and you were letting me drive.

Now I'm always steering back here.
This talking and remembering makes
me think I'm still plowing—I can feel
my hands and yours, too, on the wheel.

Connectivity

From my early childhood on the farm,
I have one memory of my father talking
on the telephone. He had some trouble
with a tractor he bought from Uncle Herb.
The problem involved the motor head.
Playing later, I pretended to be my father
on the phone. My sisters had a good laugh,
when I was overheard delivering my version
of what I thought he said, "Hello, Herb?
Can you come over and fix my head?"

Ordinarily, my father would drive
to a neighbor to talk. If he did resort
to the phone, my mother dialed the number.
After she died, though, he made his own
phone calls, but never long distance.

I called him, then, about once a month.
He'd pick up the receiver and pause
for a moment as if he needed time
to compose himself before he said, "Hello?"
His telephone voice was a little formal
and careful, but that made our talks
all the more pleasant. He seemed to say,
"This conversation is important."

One night, long after my father died,
I accidentally dialed his old number,
which was similar to one I was calling.
I realized my mistake, but I let it ring.

What if I had heard a receiver click
and a long pause? I was relieved no one
answered, but I had a good connection—
by chance, I tapped a long line of memory.
I could hear myself saying, "Hello, Herb?
Can you come over and fix my head?"

Dancing the Green
Two-Step

Cubbyholes

In cars, what most people called
the glove compartment or glove box
we called the cubbyhole, a more
inviting name, a cozy place for holding
a variety of useful and valued items.
As a child, I opened the cubbyhole
in our old Ford often, as if I expected
to find something worth looking at.

I remember seeing in there a road map
we never got far enough from home
to need, part of a broken fuel pump
from a time we got stalled, a stubby
yellow pencil, a wooden ice-cream spoon.

A few years ago, before selling my old
Monte Carlo, I checked the cubbyhole
and found, encased in a leatherette
plastic cover, the owner's manual.
I had glanced at it when the car was new.

The last time I moved, I discovered
assorted boxes and cases—cubbyholes
I had for keeping my special stuff.
Most contained useless things; some
were empty. Still, there's something
compelling about a varnished wooden box
with hinges and a latch or a cookie tin
with a cover that slides down over the top.

Now, they all seem better than anything
I ever kept in them. I could use
a good cubbyhole for cubbyholes.

What Nails Talk About
While Waiting in Their Bins

The pounding headaches
that go with the job.

When the time comes, is it better
to be driven in by many light blows
or fewer heavy ones?

Praying for a soft, yielding pine.

The possibilities of getting bent
by the dreaded glancing blow
and then having to endure
getting wrenched straight.

How wood can split and eventually
break off, leaving an exposed nail
standing there naked and useless.

The expression "Hard as nails."

Matters of faith—all service is honorable
whether it's on a palatial house
or a broken-down chicken coop,

but it's considered bad luck
to be the final nail in a coffin.

An old used nail, recycled to the bin,
doesn't talk, having suffered a trauma
when pulled out by a hammer claw.

Chicken Wisdom McNuggets

Don't count your chickens
before they're hatched,
before they cross the road,
before letting the fox guard the henhouse,
before they play a game of chicken,
before they fly the coop,
before they come home to roost,
before they run around with their heads cut off,
before the sky is falling,
and also consider this: it is better
to put all of your eggs in one basket
than to put one egg in your pants pocket.

The Farmer Marries a Mermaid

Things could work out, but getting around together
isn't easy—she rides in a water tank
in my pickup box. We talk over my shoulder
through the sliding cab window in back.
I showed her around the farm. The dry creek
was a disappointment. She liked the new
stock pond I'd dug but wasn't exactly pleased
to hear about my plans to drain the slough.
We're always talking about water—I
thought we'd sleep in a regular bed, but she
insisted we use the bathtub. We compromised
on a waterbed. Why did I marry her? Honestly,
the top half of her was so pretty, I never
considered the bottom—what was or wasn't there.

At the Café

I'm having coffee and reading
a book of poems by Emily Dickinson,
when a pesky fly buzzes
around my head and lands
beside my coffee cup.
I ask the young waitress
to please get me a flyswatter,
and she returns promptly
with a tall glass of ice water.

My laughter and lavish thanks
don't quite fit the service, and
she gives me a puzzled smile.
When I reveal the mix-up,
we both break out laughing
over the delicious rhyme.
Why didn't I see it before?
On hot summer days, we're up
to our ears in flies and ice water.

I'll leave her a large tip
for helping me make a discovery
that could prove useful if I ever
hear a fly as in Emily's line,
"I heard a Fly buzz – when I died."
I'll be forewarned to make
myself clear on my deathbed.

How Writing a Poem Is like Loading Hogs

If you get one hog headed up the chute,
the rest might follow, but sometimes not,
and you have to wrestle, shove and kick
every one of the bastards into the truck.

Short Takes

Self-Punishment

This morning my tongue hurts.
I must have bitten it during the night.
Did I say something bad in my sleep?

An Affirmative Memory

When I asked her out,
she answered, "Oh, I don't care,"
which I never regretted
taking as a "yes."

The Way it Appears

After the final season, God may be
the game's ultimate hero, but Satan
will have a better batting average.

The Prophet

I predicted I'd die before forty,
before fifty, sixty, and seventy.
I'm enjoying my failures.

No Anniversary

I had a crippling accident
fifty years ago sometime
in late August and managed
to forget the exact date.
I'm pleased in not knowing
what day not to celebrate.

Opposable Thumb in Repose

An old injury paralyzed them both.
When you open either hand, the thumb
just lies there curled up asleep
on the palm. What can you say
when a thumb's not opposable anymore?
"Come on, Thumb, it's time to get up
and meet with a finger tip. How about
a little teamwork to pick up a dime?"

You'd think a thumb would remember
how good it felt to hold the smooth
handle of a pitchfork or an axe,
or to wrap itself around the sticky
friction-taped grip of an old corn knife.

Sitting at a late-summer picnic, you ease
the neck of a cold bottle of beer
under the thumb and slide your hand
down to fit properly around the bottle.
When you cock the wrist, the thumb
tightens and holds in its sleep.
You just say, "It's all right, Thumb,
sleep on—sleep on and dream."

On the Way to Third Person

A few people I know greet me
by asking, "How is Leo today?"
It sounds as if they're asking
about someone who isn't there.
I usually answer, "I'm fine."

I've considered playing along
and saying, "He's having some pain
from his tendonitis," but that might
only encourage this line of talk.
I've felt an impulse to come back
with, "Why don't you ask him?"
But I don't really want to confront
people about how they say hello.

I wonder if there's something
about me personally that brings on
this form of greeting. What if more
of my acquaintances start saying
hello to me that way? Still, I know
that those who do are only making
a back-door attempt at humor.
I honestly like most of them.

I can live with the occasional
impersonal greeting, which I take
as an invitation to survey myself
from the outside before I end up
where I'm never either
a "You" or an "I."

Words Lost in Sleep

A nursing assistant I like
came to my room near dawn
to help me reposition.

"Were you dreaming?" she asked.
"Outside the door, I heard
you talking in your sleep.
I tried to hear what you
were saying," she confessed,
laughing, "but I couldn't."

I wished she could have heard
a memorable line or two,
but, feeling drowsy, I floated
to sleep again, pleased
she tried to listen in.

Staples

I used to keep on hand a bag
or two of dried beans, and I liked
to see several cans of beans
on a shelf or in the cupboard.
It's comforting having beans around
even when you're not eating them.

I lived alone for years, but now
that dozens of people are around
or nearby, I think of them as a kind
of staple in reserve—nursing assistants
in rooms and hallways, a nurse
passing out pills, a maintenance man
changing light bulbs, a housekeeper
with her mops and cart—they serve,
but, apart from the work they do,
their presence provides comfort.

I like that plain everyday presence,
which is like having beans plain
or in simple dishes—it's the bean taste
that counts, and there are plenty
of different beans for variety. Oh,
I don't especially care for lima beans,
but now I feel a certain comfort
when they happen to be on my plate.

Anointing the Sick

The old Franciscan priest at my door
asks if I'd like to be anointed.
I have a disability, but I'm not sick,
and I certainly don't believe
a ritual would do me any good.
It's such a cold morning, though.
The effort he must have made
to venture out strikes me
as generous and not just a habit.
It would be hard to tell him no.

He takes out a plain silver vial,
smaller than a pocket watch.
Reading some prayers, he dips
his thumb into the vial and draws
a cross with olive oil on my forehead
and on the palms of my hands.

Finished with the ceremony, he drops
the vial's cover, which rolls like a coin.
We don't see where it goes.
With difficulty, he gets on his knees
to search, saying, "I have to find it—
I couldn't easily afford another one."

I'm relieved, nearly as much as he is,
when I see and point to a silver glint
under the edge of a dresser. Grateful,
he thanks me for my good eyes,
and I thank him for stopping by.

After he leaves, I touch my forehead
with my fingers and rub my hands
as if washing them—the oil is soothing,
evidently good for my dry chapped skin.

The Fabric of Old Men

Most men at the care center
sit around in casual pants,
cotton jersey and polyester,
easy-care and lightweight.

One man has on overalls,
durable blue denim, heavy,
harder to put on, but cloth
with a heft he still needs.

Wearing light sweat pants,
I'm with the practical majority,
but I hope the man in overalls
holds out, at least for a while.

A Weather Lady

Pearl is 103 years old and living
at the care center. In the dining room,
sitting at her table by the window,
she provides reports on the weather.
After the Christmas blizzard, the drifts
almost reach the top of the window,
and she repeats every few minutes,
"There's lots of snow out there."

No wasted words about low fronts
or wind chill. "Lots of snow,"
and, following up, she predicts,
"Lots of water when that melts."
Sometimes "There's lots of sunshine,"
or "It's going to be a cloudy day."

At suppertime on winter evenings,
she says over and over again
a line that's like her signature:
"It's going to be a dark night."
Her gritty voice rises a little
on *dark* and stretches that word.
"It's going to be a *dark* night."

It's hard to tell what she's thinking,
but apparently she believes
a dark night and deep snow are two
marvels worth a lot of attention.

Better with Cream

On the farm he poured fresh cream
from a glass pitcher into his coffee.
In the nursing home after a stroke,
he picks open a tiny plastic container
of artificial creamer and pours it
onto the table—his cup isn't where
his eyes see it but farther away.
Nudging the cup closer, he tries again.
He holds and studies a creamer capsule
like a puzzle piece—you can tell
that adding the make-believe cream
is important to him even though,
when he drinks his coffee, the cup
might slip from his hand and spill.

Doc

The old podiatrist in the room
next to mine hollers a lot, at times
to get help, but often, not knowing
what he wants, he'll just launch
a series of emphatic moans,
which the nursing staff ignores.
He chants one baritone note
in rapid time, "Oh, oh, oh, oh, oh."
After awhile, there's a reversal,
in the sound, "Ho, ho, ho, ho, ho,"
(this is nothing like laughter),
and eventually the line evolves
as other letters fall into the mix,
"Whoa, whoa, whoa, whoa, whoa."
He goes on like that day and night:
"Whoa, whoa, whoa, whoa, whoa,"
as if he's hearing the steps of all
the feet in his life as hoofbeats,
or he's a farmer pulling back
on the reins of runaway horses
taking him someplace far too fast.

His Harvest

My grownup grandchildren want
to take me out to a farm to watch
threshing the old-fashioned way.
There's a field of oats in shocks,
old tractors, bundle racks, and horses.
I don't really care much to go.

I remember best going to the house
at noon with a threshing crew.
We splashed cool water on our faces
at a wash stand on the porch
and sat around the dining-room table.
My wife had worked hard all morning,
fixing fried chicken, new potatoes,
fresh vegetables from the garden,
and cherry-rhubarb pie. She poured
the coffee and joined in the talking.
To the kids it was all a big picnic.

I think about the end of a threshing day.
After the crew had gone home, the chores
still needed to be done. We had supper
late under the yellow kitchen light.
Everyone was tired without much to say.

There was the morning after threshing
was done for the year, a bright blue sky,
dew on the grass, the threshing machine
at rest beside a cottonwood tree,
and the cows turned out in the stubble.

What we wanted finished was finished,

and then one day it all ended for good.
I'd like to go back and do it over again
if sorting it all out and finding what's worth
remembering wasn't such damn hard work.

Cutting Across Pastures on My Way to School

You can sow your wheat today
is what the meadowlark says.
That's what I was told anyway.

Although we never planted wheat,
we applied the meadowlark's spring
advice to other grains like oats,

but now my farming days are gone,
I have no oats to sow, and yet
I listen to a meadowlark's song

that's wafting from the corner post
of a pasture I can only remember.
To catch the lyrics of this broadcast,

I tilt my head a certain way—
You can write your poem today.

By Hand

In those days we did everything by hand,
milked cows, pulled cockleburs, picked corn.
I wouldn't go back to that kind of work,
but it felt good, trusting my hands.

One time when I was picking corn,
at the end of the field, I led the horses
to turn the wagon around, and a pheasant
took off, exploding out of the grass.

The horses reared up, and my hand
should've let go, but it gripped the rein
tighter, and my shoulder was jerked out
of joint—remembering it still hurts,

but, Hand, I forgive you for not letting go.

Summer Green

I remember it was a hot day,
and my neighbor was wearing
a straw hat with a green eyeshade
on the front part of the brim.
I envied how the green light
dancing on his face made him
look cooler than anyone else.
Of course I could've bought
a straw hat with a green eyeshade,
but I didn't—if I had one now
and put it on, my face might feel
the light touch of a green two-step,
and I'd break out into a dance.

The Art of Perpetual Motion

A few years before he died, my father
said that sometime back in the '20s
a mechanic over by Turkey Ridge
built a perpetual motion machine.
It consisted of a wheel with weights
on hinged arms that flipped out
to provide extra leverage and torque
on the side of the wheel moving down.
This invention, according to my father,
supplied no power but did turn itself.

Moving his own arms to illustrate,
the right one extended out, the left
bent and hanging down at the elbow,
he gave a perfectly simple description
of how the device could stay in motion.

He had to be mistaken somehow,
but I didn't tell him this invention
couldn't have worked—I didn't want
to interrupt his animated description
or give a lecture on the laws of physics,
and, besides, I couldn't see exactly
why the thing wouldn't work—I gave
a little nod, a bow really, of approval,
and the pleasure I felt hasn't stopped.

ACKNOWLEGMENTS

Thanks to the editors of the following publications in which these poems first appeared.

A Harvest of Words: Contemporary South Dakota Poetry, Sioux Falls: The Center for Western Studies, Augustana College, "By Hand."

Blue Unicorn, "Reporting at My Father's Grave."

Kaleidoscope, "The Pinochle Players."

Kitchen Scraps #1, "Dakota Wind."

The Rockford Review, "My First Memory of Dancing."

Paddlefish, "A Farming Life," "Connectivity," "Essentials of Comedy," "Independent Harvesters," "Saving Singletrees," "She Remembers His Overalls."

Slant, "Anointing the Sick."

South Dakota Magazine, "Starting the Day," "Seasons of Harmony," "The Evidence of Pleasure."

Third Wednesday, "Convergence," "Doc," "Grocery String," "Cutting Across Pastures on My Way to School," "The Girl I Saw at a Movie," "What They Carried," "Screech Owl," "Lights," "It," "The Fabric of Old Men," "What Nails Talk About While Waiting in Their Bins," "Summer Green," "The Art of Perpetual Motion." Special thanks to the editors of *TW* for honoring me as the featured poet in their fall 2012 issue.

About the Author

Leo Dangel, the great-grandson of German and Danish homesteaders, was born in South Dakota and grew up on a farm near Freeman and Turkey Ridge. After receiving an MA from Emporia State University in Kansas, he taught at Southwest Minnesota State University in Marshall until his retirement as an emeritus professor of English. He now lives in Yankton, South Dakota. His poems have appeared in many anthologies and periodicals including *Great River Review, The Midwest Quarterly, North Dakota Quarterly, Plainsong, Commonweal, Paddlefish, Zone 3,* and *Nebraska Territory.* He was awarded The Elkhorn Prize and was twice a finalist in the Minnesota Book Awards. His poems have been read frequently on Garrison Keillor's *The Writer's Almanac,* and have appeared in Ted Kooser's *American Life in Poetry* column. In 1998, The Lyric Theater of Minneapolis staged a revue of Leo Dangel poems, *Old Man Brunner Country,* which continues to be performed in revivals.

Books by Leo Dangel

Keeping Between the Fences, (chapbook), Westerheim Press, 1981.

Old Man Brunner Country, Spoon River Poetry Press, 1987.

Hogs and Personals, Spoon River Poetry Press, 1992.

Home from the Field: Collected Poems, Spoon River Poetry Press, 1997.

The Crow on the Golden Arches, Spoon River Poetry Press, 2004.

Saving Singletrees, WSC Press, 2013.

ABOUT THE KLOEFKORN SERIES

The Kloefkorn Series cuts across every genre, snatching books that embody creativity, originality, and a new way of looking at something—traits we look for in every book we read, and find less often than we wish. All of our authors have at least one foot in the Great Plains, whether they like it or not.

Before his death, William Kloefkorn gracefully and generously granted us permission to use his name for our book series, on the guarantee that hc would gct a sncak peek at whatever we're publishing. We know for a fact we got the better end of the deal.

Proclaimed Nebraska State Poet in 1982, William Kloefkorn (August 12, 1932 to May 19, 2011) was the author of more than thirty books of poetry, fiction and memoir, including *Swallowing the Soap* (2010), *Drinking the Tin Cup Dry* (1989), *Restoring the Burnt Child* (2003), *A Time to Sink Her Pretty Little Ship* (1999) and *Out of Attica* (2008), just to name a few. His writing frequently celebrated rural life and the landscape of the Great Plains. Kloefkorn was also the first-place winner of the 1978 Nebraska Hog-Calling Championship, an amazing yodeler, and an emeritus professor of English at Nebraska Wesleyan University. William Kloefkorn, more than any other American poet, brought the value of poetry and literature to Nebraska. An avid believer in people and education, he never said "no" to furthering the encouragement of the arts and always took the time to tell the stories that inspired generations of poets and writers. He knew how to make each one of us feel special to him and to ourselves. Along with his biggest supporter, his wife, Eloise, his baritone voice circled beautiful stories, creating many privileged occasions in elementary and high schools, college campuses, bars, on the prairies and around the country for all kinds of people to explore their work and themselves.

And, as Tim Black said, William Kloefkorn is the grandfather of every Nebraskan poet.

The Kloefkorn Series was the brainchild of Cynthia and Timothy Black, with encouragement and help from J.V. Brummels in honor of their friend William Kloefkorn. This creative maelstrom is always and forever dedicated to them.

For more information about the series:
wsc.edu/wscpress/Kloefkorn/

OTHER KLOEFKORN SERIES BOOKS

1
Connecticut Shade by Timothy Black

2
Roadside Prophet by Grizz McIntosh

3
Jeweled Fragments by Ron Vick, Sr.

4
Songs from Our Summer by Max McElwain

5
Requiem for the Kid on Grand Piano by Johnny D. Iles

6
The ABC's of Dinkology by Aaron Stueve

7
Undoing Orion's Belt by Amy Plettner

8
The Music Box Treaty by Richard Duggin